Strong's Book of Designs; a Masterpiece of Modern Ornamental Art

TT360
.S92
1917

34

440

BOOK OF DESIGNS

BY

C'J'Strong

EASTER

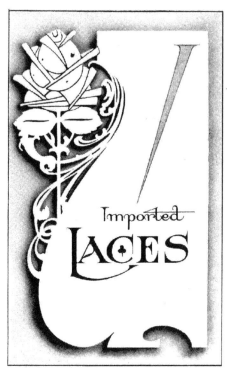

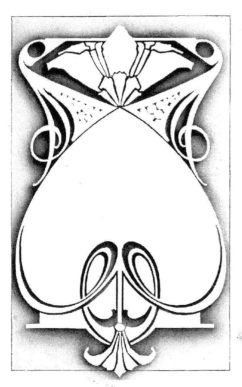
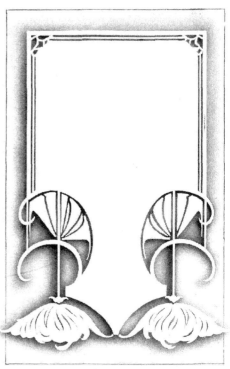

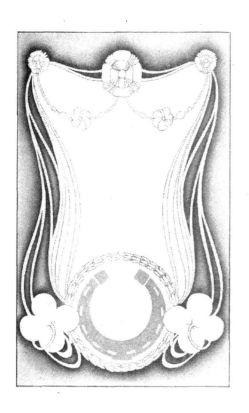

SPORTING GOODS

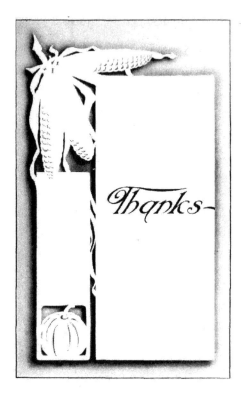

Thanks-

-giving..

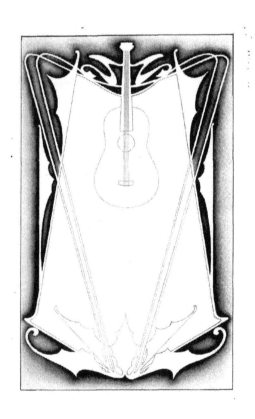

THE COSY THEATRE
HOLIDAY BILL

MIDGET THEATRE
Attractions

HAVE A LOOK FOR
10

MODERN STYLES LETTER DECORATION

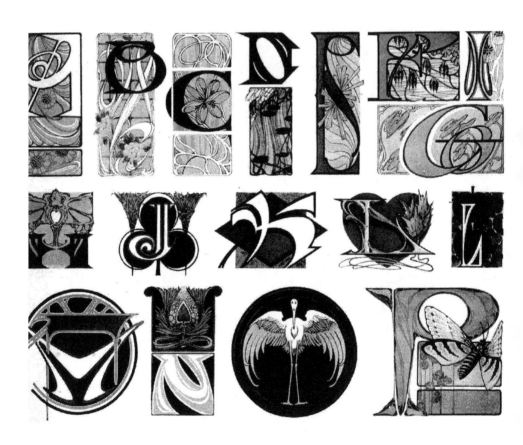

SMITH WILL SIGN ANYTHING
CALL ME UP
121 Blank St
BIGTOWN N. Y.

Smith will SIGN anything
121 BLANK ST.
BIGTOWN, N.Y.
CALL HIM UP

Business Cards

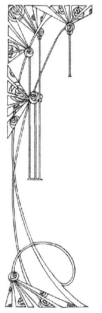

SMITH & SMITH

SIGN PAINTERS

PHONE
2002

121 BLANK ST. BIGTOWN N.Y.

MAIN
FLOOR

SMITH & SMITH

SIGNS

PHONE
2002

MAIN
FLOOR

121 BLANK ST.   BIGTOWN N.Y.

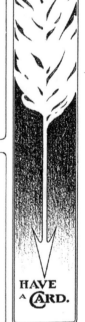

HAVE
A CARD.

Peculiar Decoration.

Odds and Ends

1910

Practical Ornamentation

WOLVERINE

Automobile Company

Detroit ✦ ✦ ✦ Michigan

HIGH GRADE AUTOMOBILES

Wolverine
Automobiles
General Purpose
Touring Cars and
Runabouts

We make 'em   while you wait.

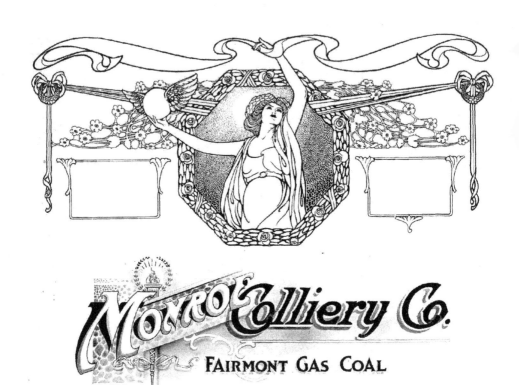

Monro Colliery Co.

FAIRMONT GAS COAL

EUREKA SHARPENER COMPANY

MANUFACTURERS OF
LAWN MOWER
SHARPENERS

S. O. Mannausa PRINTING CO.

50-52-54 TENTH ST.

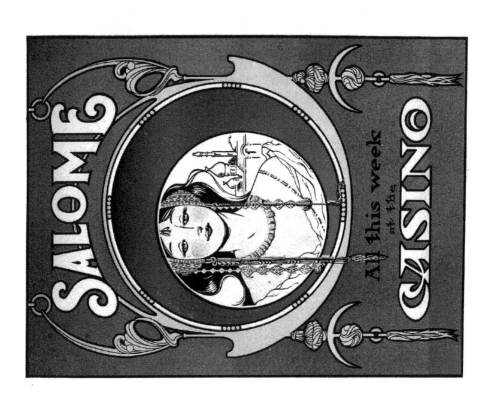

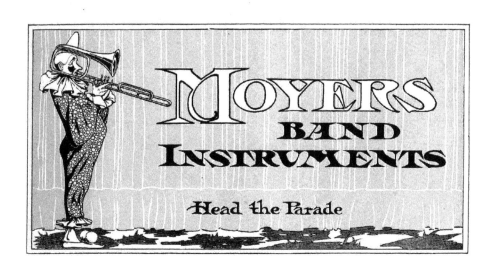

MOYERS
BAND
INSTRUMENTS

Head the Parade

RIBBONS

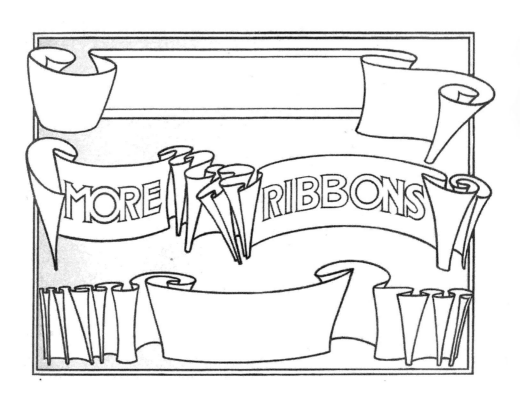

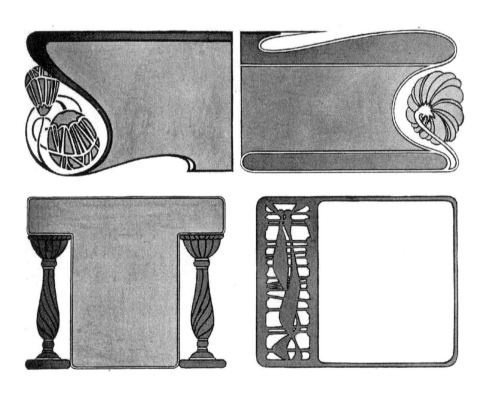

PANELS

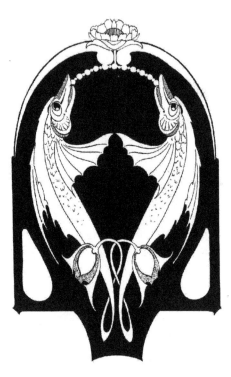

SLEEPY

OR LIFE OF A BOY IN A SIGN SHOP

by
I. Ben There.

THE
GOOD
OLD
SUM-
MER
TIME

By S. PLUNK

ECCENTRIC
PANELS

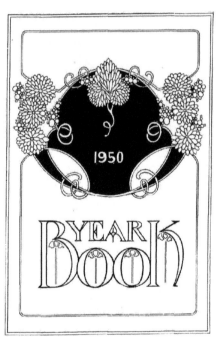

1950

YEAR
BOOK

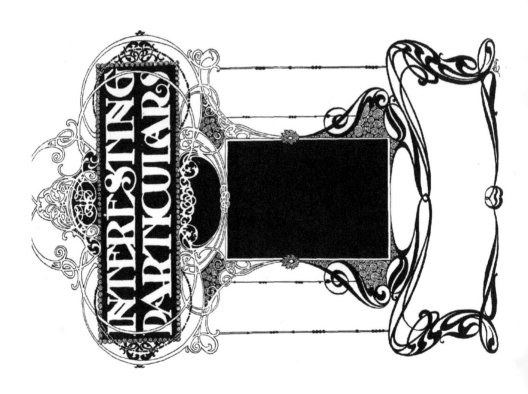

INTERESTING PARTICULARS

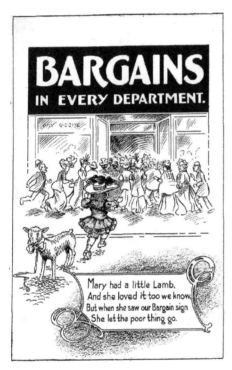

Daily
BARGAIN
BULLETIN.

MENS *Fleece* **SUITS**
Lined
Riveted
Buttons
Warm &
Cool.

Marked down
from $10. to **10¢**

A **FACT**
that
sounds like a
JEST!

All wool
double-
story

COLLARS
1¢ *each*

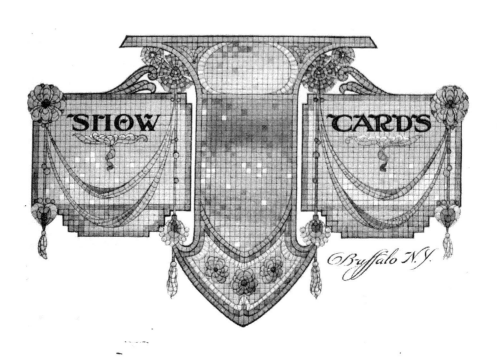

SHOW CARDS

Buffalo N.Y.

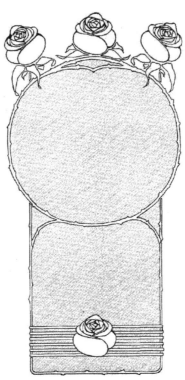

FINE FLOWERS MAKE FINE HATS

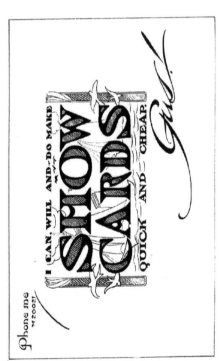

Good Music 5¢

There & Back Ten Cents.

SKATING at Belle Isle

BULLETIN & DESIGNS

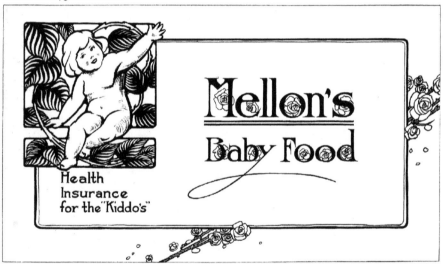

Mellon's
Baby Food

Health
Insurance
for the "Kiddo's"

CARD ❦ IDEAS

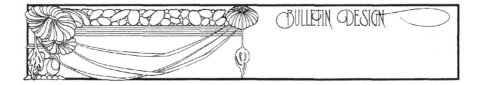

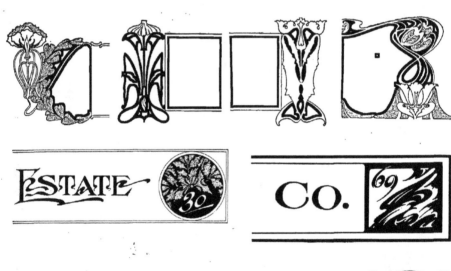

ABCD
EFGHIJKL
MNOPRST
UVWXYZ

ABC
DEFGHI
JKLMNOPQ
RSTUV
WXYZ

ABCD
EFGHIJKL
MNOPRST
UVWXYZ

ABC
DEFGHIJ
KLMNOP
RSTUV
WXYZ

ABCD
EFGHIJKL
MNOPRST
UVWXYZ

ABCDEFG
HIJKLMN
OPRSTUV
WXYZ
123456789

ABCD

EFGHIJKL

MNOPRST

UVWXYZ

ABCD
EFGHIJKL
MNOPRST
UVWXYZ

ABCDEF
GHIJKLMN
OPPRSST
UVOXYE
abcdefghhijklmnn
opqrstfaavwxyzz

CPSIA information can be obtained
at www.ICGtesting.com
Printed in the USA
BVHW060035100920
588456BV00003B/163